The PHANTOM of the OPERA

Music by ANDREW LLOYD WEBBER
Lyrics by CHARLES HART
Additional lyrics by RICHARD STILGOE
Title song: lyrics by CHARLES HART,
Additional lyrics by RICHARD STILGOE & MIKE BATT
Book by RICHARD STILGOE & ANDREW LLOYD WEBBER

The Phantom played by MICHAEL CRAWFORD
Christine played by SARAH BRIGHTMAN   Raoul played by STEVE BARTON

You must be always
on your guard,
or he will catch you with his
magical lasso!

He's here:
the Phantom of the Opera . . .

And in
this labyrinth,
where night is blind,
the Phantom of the Opera
is there —
inside my mind . . .

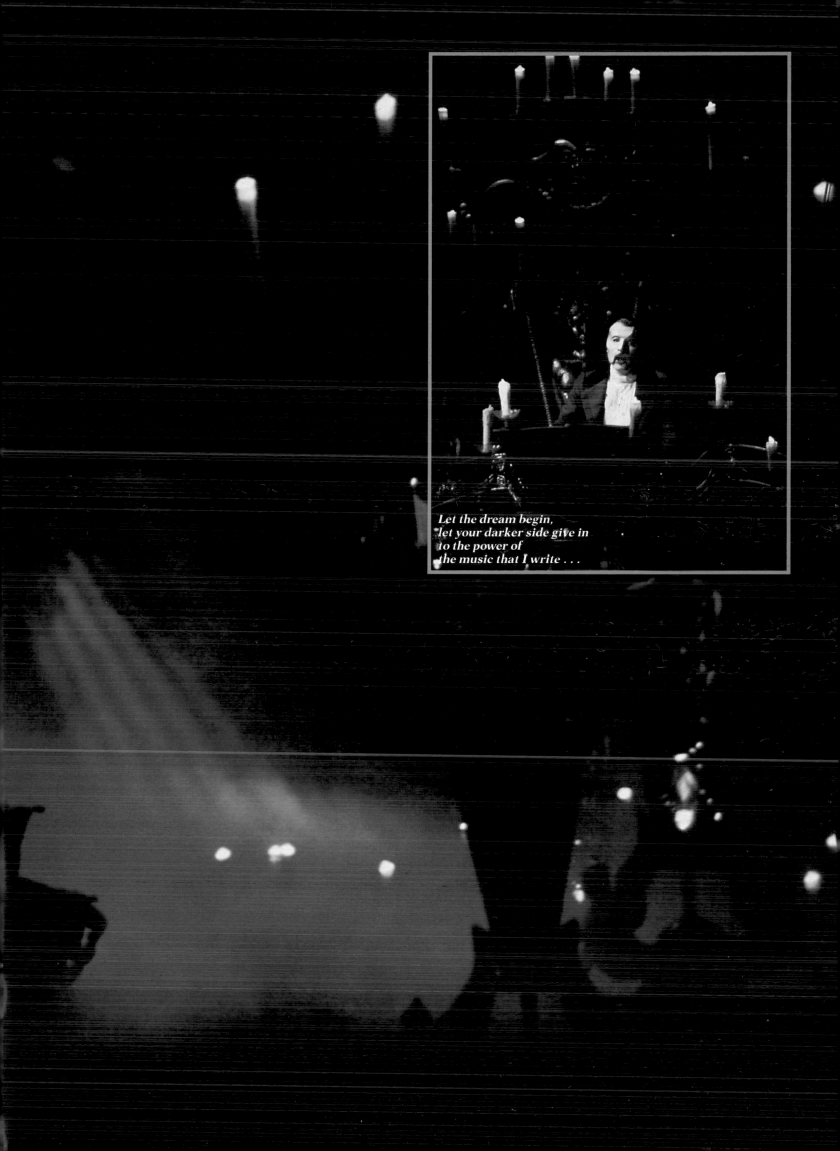

*Let the dream begin,
let your darker side give in
to the power of
the music that I write . . .*

Behold! She is singing to bring down the chandelier!

I advise you to comply —
my instructions should be clear —
Remember,
there are worse things
than a shattered chandelier . . .

Masquerade!
Stop and stare
at the sea of smiles
around you!

Have you missed me, good messieurs?
I have written you an opera!

The world forgot him,
but I never can . . .
For in this darkness
I have seen him again . . .

In sleep
he sang to me,
in dreams
he came . . .
that voice
which calls to me
and speaks
my name . . .

You alone
can make my song take flight . . .

Fear can
turn to love — you'll
learn to see, to
find the man
behind the monster . . .

Andrew Lloyd Webber was born in 1948. He is the composer of *Joseph And The Amazing Technicolor Dreamcoat* (1968) (extended 1972), *Jesus Christ Superstar* (1971), the film scores of *Gumshoe* (1971) and *The Odessa File* (1973), *Jeeves* (1974), *Evita* (1976), *Variations* (1978) and *Tell Me On A Sunday* (1979) combined as *Song And Dance* (1982), *Cats* (1981), *Starlight Express* (1984) and *Requiem*, a setting of the Latin Requiem Mass (1985). Mr Lloyd Webber's awards include three Tonys and the Grammy Award for Best Classical Contemporary Composition for *Requiem* in 1986. *The Phantom of the Opera* won 'Best Musical of 1986' in both the Laurence Olivier and Evening Standard Drama Awards. He is married to Sarah Brightman.

Charles Hart was born in 1961 and educated at Desborough School, Maidenhead, Robinson College, Cambridge and the Guildhall School, London. His first compositions were heard while he was still at school, and he appeared in some thirteen plays, musicals and operas while at university, where he also wrote words and music for a variety of songs and one (unperformed) musical, *Moll Flanders*. Since leaving the Guildhall, where he studied composition with Robert Saxton, he has worked as a keyboard player, répétiteur and vocal coach in the West End. *The Phantom of the Opera* marks his début as a professional stage writer.

Richard Stilgoe has a wife, an ex-wife, five children, a dog and a Hymac digger. From this you will gather that he is passionate and creative but essentially down to earth. He was born in Camberley and brought up in Liverpool, where he sang 'I Know That My Redeemer Liveth' at St. Agnes' Church and 'Rip It Up' at the Cavern. In trying to write a song as good as either of these, he has now written several hundred, and played the results on radio *(Today, Stilgoe's Around* and the prize-winning *Hamburger Weekend)*, on television *(Nationwide, That's Life*, his own series and everyone else's) and on stages all over the world. His one-man show has been seen at festivals from Edinburgh to Adelaide. Clients for his bespoke cabaret act include IBM in Rhodes, Butlin's in Toronto and H.M. The Queen at Windsor Castle. His two-man show with Peter Skellern ran happily in London's West End, and is soon to be seen on Broadway. For Andrew Lloyd Webber he co-wrote with Trevor Nunn the words for the opening song of *Cats*, and all of the words in *Starlight Express*. This has paid for the Hymac digger, and enabled him to found the Orpheus Trust, which helps disabled children to play and enjoy music. Much of his work is now with children. He has his own BBC 1 children's series, introduces opera to children at Glyndebourne and is a patron of the National Youth Music Theatre, for whom he is currently writing the words and music of *Bodywork*, a musical that takes place inside the human body. This has its première at the 1987 Brighton Festival, before going on to Edinburgh. He still occasionally sings 'Rip It Up', but now finds 'I Know That My Redeemer Liveth' a bit high.

THINK OF ME

Music by ANDREW LLOYD WEBBER
Lyrics by CHARLES HART
Additional lyrics by RICHARD STILGOE

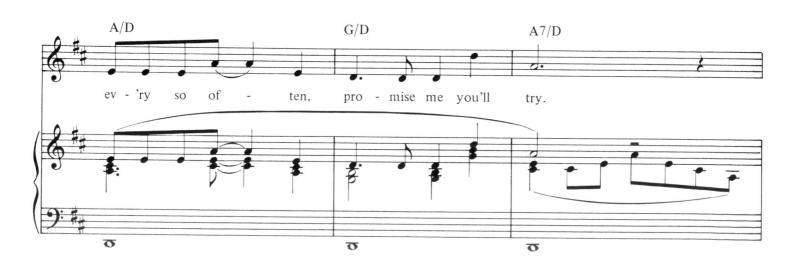

On that day,___ that not so dis-tant day,___ when you are far a-way and free, if you ev-er find a mo-ment, spare a thought for me.

And though it's clear,___ though it was al-ways clear___ that this was

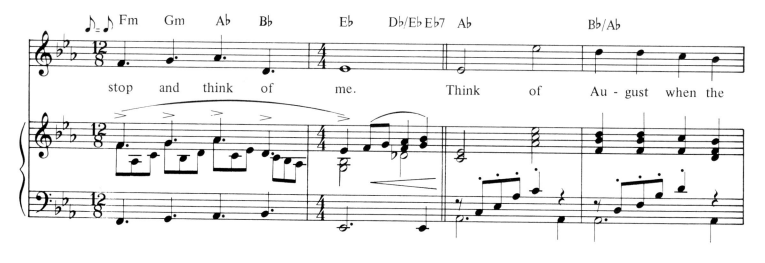

nev-er meant to be, if you hap-pen to re-mem-ber,

stop and think of me. Think of Au-gust when the

trees were green; don't think a-bout the way things

day   when   I   won't   think   of   you.

RAOUL

Can it be,

can it be Christ - ine?   Long a - go,___ it seems so

long a - go,___ how young and in - no - cent we were.   She may not re - mem - ber

14

ANGEL OF MUSIC

Music by ANDREW LLOYD WEBBER
Lyrics by CHARLES HART
Additional lyrics by RICHARD STILGOE

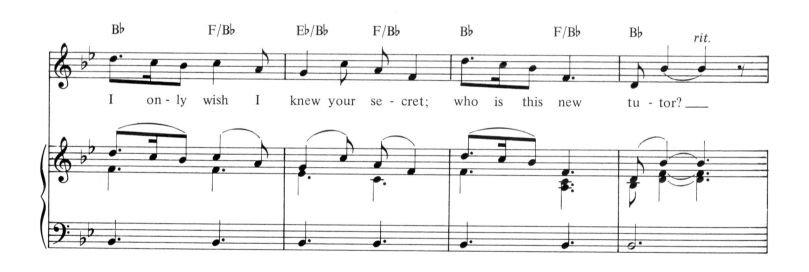

An - gel, my soul was weak; for-give me! En - ter at last, mas-ter! ____

PHANTOM

Flat-ter - ing child, you shall know me, ___ see why in sha-dow I hide.

Look at your face in the mir - ror! ___ I am there in - side.

CHRISTINE

An - gel of mu - sic, guide and guar-dian, grant to me your glo - ry! _____

THE PHANTOM OF THE OPERA

Music by ANDREW LLOYD WEBBER
Lyrics by CHARLES HART
Additional lyrics by RICHARD STILGOE & MIKE BATT

phan - tom of the op-er-a is here _____ in - side my
phan - tom of the op-er-a is there _____ in - side your

mind.
mind.

PHANTOM *(Spoken)* Sing, my angel of music!

CHRISTINE He's

there the phan - tom of the op - era. _____

Ah! _____

PHANTOM Sing, my angel, sing!

28

*Think of me,
think of me fondly
when we've said
goodbye . . .*

Softly, deftly,
music shall caress you . . .
Hear it, feel it
secretly possess you . . .

THE MUSIC OF THE NIGHT

Music by ANDREW LLOYD WEBBER
Lyrics by CHARLES HART
Additional lyrics by RICHARD STILGOE

night un-furls its splen-dour; grasp it, sense it, trem-u-lous and ten-der.

Turn your face a-way from the gar-ish light of day, turn your thoughts a-way from cold, un feel ing

light and lis-ten to the mu-sic of the night. Close your eyes and sur-ren-der to your

dark-est dreams! Purge your thoughts of the life you knew be - fore! Close your

night. Let your mind start a jour-ney through a strange, new world; leave all

thoughts of the world you knew be - fore. Let your soul take you where you long to

be! On - ly then can you be - long to me.

Float-ing, fall - ing, sweet in-tox-i-ca - tion. Touch me, trust me, sa-vour each sen-sa - tion.

PRIMA DONNA

Music by ANDREW LLOYD WEBBER
Lyrics by CHARLES HART
Additional lyrics by RICHARD STILGOE

more! _____

CARLOTTA

Pri - ma Don - na, your song ___ shall live a - gain, ___ you took a snub, ___ but there's a pub - lic who needs you. _____ Think of their cry of un - dy - ing ___ sup - port, fol - low where the lime - light

ANDRÉ & FIRMIN

more! _____ Who'd be-lieve a di-va hap-py to re-lieve a cho-rus girl who's gone and slept with the pa-tron?_ Raoul and the soub-rette en-twined in love's du-et; al-though he may de-mur he must have been with her. You'd nev-er get a-way with all this in a play, but if it's loud-ly sung and in a for-eign tongue, it's just the sort of sto-ry au-dien-ces a-dore, in

MELODY

fact, a per - fect op - era. Pri - ma Don - na, the world __ is at your feet, a na - tion waits __ and how it hates to be cheat - ed. ___ Light up the stage with that age old __ rap - port; ___ sing, __ Pri - ma __ Don - na, once

ALL I ASK OF YOU

Music by ANDREW LLOYD WEBBER
Lyrics by CHARLES HART
Additional lyrics by RICHARD STILGOE

No more talk of dark-ness, for-get these wide-eyed fears; I'm
here, noth-ing can harm you, my words will warm and calm you.
Let me be your free-dom, let day-light dry your tears; I'm

here, with you, be-side you, to guard you and to guide you.

CHRISTINE

All I ask is ev-ery wak-ing mo-ment, turn my head with talk of sum-mer-time.__ Say you need me with you now and al-ways; pro-mise me that all you say is true, that's all I ask of

MASQUERADE

Music by ANDREW LLOYD WEBBER
Lyrics by CHARLES HART
Additional lyrics by RICHARD STILGOE

Mas-quer-ade, _____ pa - per fa - ces on par-ade.

Mas - quer-ade, ___ hide your face so the world will nev - er find you. Mas-quer-ade, ____ ev-ery

sea of smiles a-round you. Mas-quer-ade, seeth-ing sha-dows, breath-ing lies,

mas - quer-ade _____ you can fool an - y friend who ev - er knew you.

Mas-quer-ade, _____ leer-ing sa-tyrs, peer-ing eyes,

mas - quer-ade, _____ run and hide, but a

face will still pur-sue you. What a night, what a crowd, makes you glad, makes you proud, all the

What I once used to dream
I now dread . . .
if he finds me, it won't
ever end . . .

*We've passed the point
of no return . . .*

WISHING YOU WERE SOMEHOW
HERE AGAIN

Music by ANDREW LLOYD WEBBER
Lyrics by CHARLES HART
Additional lyrics by RICHARD STILGOE

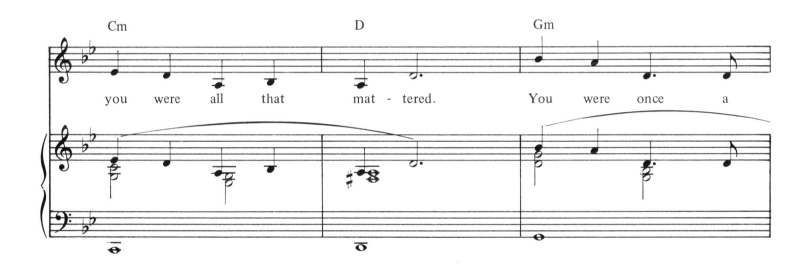

THE POINT OF NO RETURN

Music by ANDREW LLOYD WEBBER
Lyrics by CHARLES HART
Additional lyrics by RICHARD STILGOE

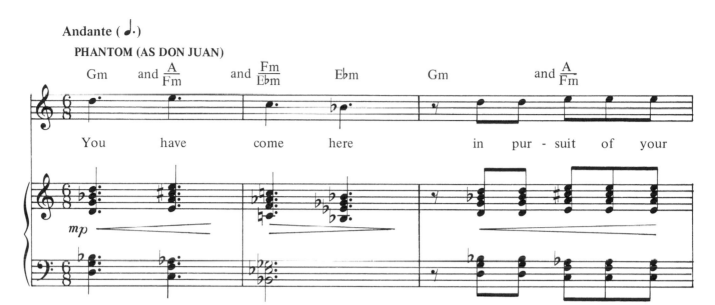

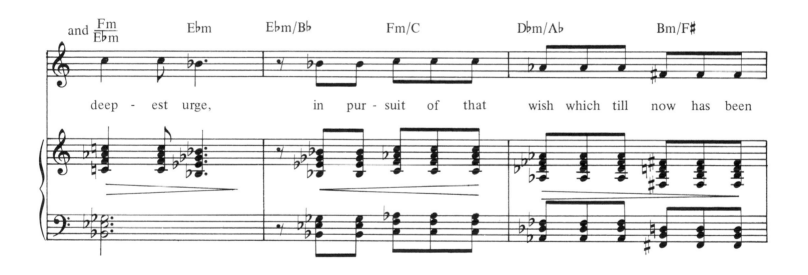

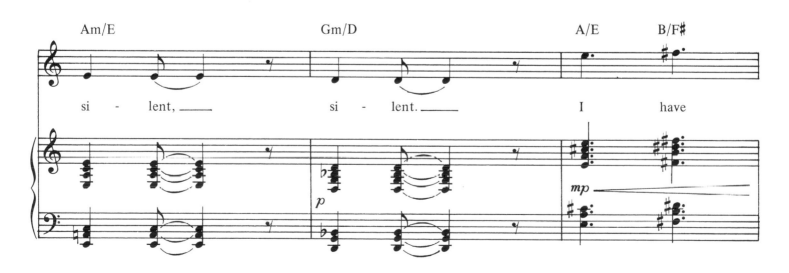

an - don thought and let the dream des - cend.

What rag - ing fire shall flood the soul? What rich de -

sire un - locks its door? What sweet se - duc - tion lies be -

fore us? Past _____ the point of

no re-turn, the fi-nal thre-shold, what
warm un-spok-en se-crets will we learn be-
yond the point of no re-turn?

CHRISTINE (AS AMINTA)
You have brought me to that mo-ment where

gun.　　Past　　all thought of right　or wrong,

one fi - nal ques - tion:　　how　long should　we　two

wait　be-fore we're one?　　When will　the　blood be - gin to

race? The sleep-ing　bud burst in-to　bloom? When will　the　flames at last con-

EXCLUSIVELY DISTRIBUTED BY

HAL•LEONARD™
CORPORATION

7777 W. BLUEMOUND RD. P.O. BOX 13819 MILWAUKEE, WI 53213

Exclusive Distributors:
Hal Leonard Publishing Corporation
8112 W. Bluemond Road, P.O. 13819 Milwaukee, Wisconsin 53213.
Music Sales Limited
8/9 Frith Street, London W1V 5TZ, England.

This book © Copyright 1987 by The Really Useful Group plc
Inventory No. 00360830
ISBN 0-88188-615-7

Arranged by Roger Day
Photographs by Clive Barda
Music engraving by Music Print Ltd.
Cover artwork by Dewynters Limited, London.

World première at Her Majesty's Theatre
Thursday October 9th, 1986.